FUTURE TRANSPORT
IN SPACE

By Steve Parker

Illustrations by David West

 **Marshall Cavendish**
Benchmark

New York

This edition first published in 2012 in the United States by
Marshall Cavendish Benchmark

An imprint of Marshall Cavendish Corporation

Website: www.marshallcavendish.us

This publication represents the opinions and views of the author based on Steve Parker's personal experience, knowledge, and research. The information in this book serves as a general guide only. The author and publisher have used their best efforts in preparing this book, and disclaim liability rising directly and indirectly from the use and application of this book.

Other Marshall Cavendish Offices:
Marshall Cavendish International (Asia) Private Limited, 1 New Industrial Road, Singapore 536196 • Marshall Cavendish International (Thailand) Co Ltd. 253 Asoke, 12th Flr, Sukhumvit 21 Road, Klongtoey Nua, Wattana, Bangkok 10110, Thailand • Marshall Cavendish (Malaysia) Sdn Bhd, Times Subang, Lot 46, Subang Hi-Tech Industrial Park, Batu Tiga, 40000 Shah Alam, Selangor Darul Ehsan, Malaysia

Marshall Cavendish is a trademark of Times Publishing Limited

Copyright © 2011 David West Children's Books

Library of Congress Cataloging-in-Publication Data

Parker, Steve, 1952-
In space / Steve Parker.
p. cm. -- (Future transport)
Includes index.
Summary: "Gives a concise history of travel by land, water, air, or in space, showing the technology available today, in the near future, and in centuries to come"--Provided by publisher.
ISBN 978-1-60870-778-2 (print)
1. Space colonies--Juvenile literature. 2. Astronautics--Juvenile literature. 3. Outer space--Exploration--Juvenile literature. I. Title.
TL795.7.P37 2012
629.4--dc22

2011001130

Produced by
David West 🏃🏃 Children's Books
7 Princeton Court
55 Felsham Road
London SW15 1AZ

Designer: Gary Jeffrey
Illustrator: David West

The photographs in this book are used by permission and through the courtesy of:
Abbreviations: t-top, m-middle, b-bottom, r-right, l-left, c-center.
Title page, 6m, 6r, 7t, 8b, 10l, 11t, 11m, 12bl, 13tr, 14-15, 14t, 14b, 15t, 15m, 16all, 17l, 17t, 17m, 18all, 19bl, 19br, 20r, 20b, 22all, 23t, 23br, 26t, 28all, 30t, NASA; 6t, SpaceX, 6l, 12t, US Air Force; 8t, NASA/Crew of STS-79, 8l, ESA/D.Ducros; 9tr, NASA Ames Research Center, 9l, 11bl, 19br, NASA Marshall Space Flight Center Collection; 10t, NASA Dryden, 10b, Reaction Engine Ltd; 11mr, EADS Astrium; 12br, DARPA; 15b, Jürgen Matern; 17b, 20l, 23m, ESA; 19l, Richard Kurbis; 20tr, EADS Astrium/ESA; 21t, NASA Goddard Photo and Video; 23bl, NASA/Carla Cioffi; 24t, Excalibur Almaz Limited, 24l, Mark Greenberg/Virgin Galactic; 25t, courtesy of Armadillo Aerospace, 25m, Mike Massee / XCOR, 25r, Space Exploration Technologies Corp; 26br, Eric Erbe, digital colorization by Christopher Pooley, both of USDA, ARS, EMU, 26b, NASA-JSC

Printed in China
135642

Contents

INTRODUCTION

"Welcome to Spaceport Beta. Would passengers for the Moon Shuttle please go to Dock 4. The arrival of Mars SuperCruiser 776 has been delayed by thirty-nine hours due to a cosmic ray storm. Freightliner M41 from the platinum mine on asteroid Psyche is due at Dock 16B. Travelers for the Saturn Rings Tour must check their hibernation suits before departure. Have a great trip!"

Space is the great future challenge for transport and travel. Yet even a simple space mission costs millions of dollars. Distances are vast—going to the closest planets takes months. Today's technology will have to advance hugely for spaceships and space trips to be as common as air flights now.

Yet just fifty years ago, exploring space had hardly begun. Who knows what lies ahead in our quest for travel to the stars?

FUTURE LAUNCH

Most people call them "space rockets" but they are better known as launch vehicles. In years to come, they may not have rocket engines at all.

SpaceX's Falcon 1 was developed by a private company, not a government. In 2009 it launched its first customer's satellite.

For small loads, Boeing Delta IV launchers use only the central vehicle with its Rocketdyne RS-68 engine. Extra boosters give more lift for heavy cargoes.

HEAVY LIFTERS

Launch vehicles, LVs, have so much power that they can reach escape velocity, which is 7 miles (11 km) each second, to break free of Earth's gravity. Small LVs carry a satellite or two into space. Heavy-lift LVs weigh over 2,000 tons (1,800 t) and raise more than 100 tons (90 t) into orbit.

Ares 1 (right), a U.S. launcher canceled due to budget cuts, may be reborn as the new Liberty rocket.

A system of flyback, reusable boosters is being developed with help from the second man on the Moon, Buzz Aldrin.

"Seemed like a good idea..."
Science fiction author Jules Verne described a "moon gun" in his story From the Earth to the Moon (1865). It shot a spacecraft like a ball from a giant cannon. But the sudden force from speeding up so fast would kill the travelers at once.

Mass Drivers

One alternative to a rocket engine may be the mass driver or electro-catapult. It works like a superspeed maglev train, using powerful electrical magnets to speed a launch vehicle faster and faster, shooting up and away into space.

Next-generation airports may have spaceport terminals, too. Launch vehicles not only take off vertically, straight up, but also land vertically, straight down.

A Moon-based mass driver would hurl launch vehicles along a lengthy track and up into space.

SPACE BASE

The first successful Earth-orbit space station was Russia's *Salyut 3* in 1974. Today the *ISS, International Space Station*, is twenty times bigger with room for six crew. What will tomorrow's homes in space look like?

The Russian Mir space station was inhabited from 1986 to 2001. Then It burned up as a fireball on re-entry.

The Jules Verne ATV (Automated Transfer Vehicle) is a robot "space tug" that carries supplies up to the ISS. Its first mission was in 2008 and several more ATVs are planned.

MODULAR DESIGN

The Salyuts, U.S.'s *Skylab*, and other early space bases were one-piece. The *ISS* is modular, with sections or modules carried up by launchers such as Soyuz, and then fixed together in orbit. Electricity comes from vast solar panels with an area more than half an American football field.

Building the ISS began on Earth in 1990, and in orbit in 1998. With more than twenty main parts or modules, its life should extend beyond 2020.

GENERATING GRAVITY

In the *ISS* the crew float around weightless. The next advance could be a modular ring-shaped space station that spins around. The spinning would produce a centrifugal force that would feel like gravity here on Earth. This space base might be a jumping-off place for faraway planets.

"Seemed like a good idea..."

Back in the 1970s, the U.S. space agency NASA asked artists and scientists to imagine future scenes. One result was a giant circular "space farm" where crops thrived away from Earth's pollution in much brighter sunlight and warmth.

A space elevator will have an enormously long rope or tether from the spinning Earth's surface to a counterweight orbiting in space. Elevator cars ride up and down the cable.

Robot supply ship

Soyuz transport craft

Solar panel

Core module

Inflatable BA 300 module

BA 330

SPACE MOTEL

2020 could see *Bigelow's* modular "space motel." Living and working areas are based on BA 300 units launched in a collapsed form, and blown up to full size in space with compressed gases.

Spaceplanes

The North American X-15 was an experimental rocket plane that blasted to the edge of space, more than 67 miles (108 km) high, in 1963.

Launch vehicles may continue to carry big loads into space. But a neater idea might be a spaceplane. It will take off and land like an aircraft, but also go much higher, into orbit and perhaps beyond.

Return Tickets

Spaceplanes would prevent the huge waste of many launch vehicles, which take their payloads into space and then drift away useless into the emptiness. These new craft could make many trips up and down, either sub-orbital "hops" just into space and back, or entering full Earth orbit.

The U.S. space shuttles flew from 1981 to 2011. They were a type of reusable spaceplane but needed extra rocket boosters for take-off and glided down to land.

The unmanned Skylon proposal has a jet engine that uses oxygen from the air while low down, then liquid oxygen from its own tank in space. It could take 12 tons (11 t) into orbit, fly back to its runway and refuel for the next mission.

10

NASA's X-43 robot scramjet test plane, just 12 feet (3.7 m) long, reached more than 7,500 mph (12,000 km/h) in 2004. But it had to be boosted by a rocket to a speed where the scramjet started working.

Air intake

Liquid hydrogen injected

Combustion

Exhaust gives thrust

HOW SCRAMJETS WORK

The scramjet has no moving parts—no spinning turbines to suck in and compress air, like a normal jet. It relies on its own incredible speed, usually over 1,000 mph (1,600 km/h), to "ram" air into it at high enough pressure to squeeze and burn the fuel.

"Seemed like a good idea..."

In the 1970s, VentureStar was supposed to bring the Space Age to ordinary travelers with joyrides into orbit. After more than $1.2 billion, several test failures of scaled-down models, and lack of interest, it was canceled.

Astrium's hybrid tourist space-plane looks like a business jet.

HYBRIDS

When fuel burns it combines with oxygen or an oxidizer chemical. Oxygen is plentiful in the air of Earth's atmosphere, but in space there is no air (or anything else). Hybrid spaceplanes will use jet engines low down, then rockets with their own oxidizer supply in space.

Aerospike rockets shoot their thrust down a narrowing angled ridge rather than out of the usual nozzle. Test flights could begin soon.

11

STAR WARS

We love movies about heroic humans battling alien invaders from distant galaxies. But could space be the ultimate battle scene for powers based here on Earth?

The U.S.'s Prompt Global Strike idea combines orbiting missile bases with ground- and ship-launched cruise missiles. PGS could hit any target on Earth within one hour.

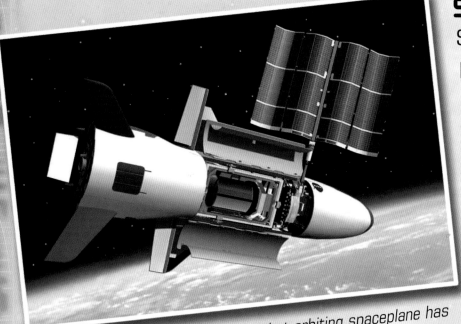

Boeing's X-37 robot orbiting spaceplane has been testing military roles since 2010.

SPIES IN SPACE

Satellites carry amazingly powerful cameras, infrared or heat sensors, movement detectors, and other equipment, to spot tanks, missiles, combat planes, and warships. They also monitor radio and microwave messages from possible enemies. Almost nothing can be hidden from these silent spies in space.

ORBITAL RAILGUN

The railgun uses electrical and magnetic forces to speed an object between railway-type metal tracks. The object could be a spy satellite or explosives from a space weapon.

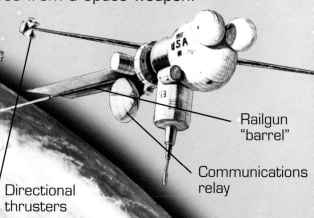

Directional thrusters

Railgun "barrel"

Communications relay

Railgun tests in the U.S. have fired test "bullets" at more than 6,000 mph (9,700 km/h), leaving a trail of superheated gases called plasma.

Plans for the space combat craft X-20 Dyna Soar *began in 1957 with designs and models. But in 1963, after $5 billion (in today's costs), and just as building the real spacecraft began, it was canceled.*

BOILED INTO BITS

Rocket-propelled missiles with exploding warheads could work in space. But much faster would be super-power lasers. The laser light beam needs enough energy to heat its target so quickly that it boils and blasts itself apart.

From successful tests on laser weapons done here on Earth, scientists calculate that one space laser could seek and destroy up to twenty enemy satellites and weapons.

Satellites could carry space "battlebots"—self-propelled remote-guided exploding robots.

Moon Town

With today's rockets and spacecraft, the Moon is almost three days away. But faster forms of propulsion could shorten the trip to a few hours, and make the Moon a great jumping-off place to reach the planets and stars.

NASA's Altair is one of the stages in the development of future Moon soft-landers.

FUTURE FRONTIER

One of the Moon's attractions is that it has less attraction—its gravity pull is only one-seventh of Earth's. Launch vehicles blasting off from there would be much smaller and more efficient. Also useful minerals on the Moon could be mined to build living bases and spacecraft. Recent discoveries show that there is even some water. The Moon could become home away from home.

Solar panels could make electricity for Moon observatories to study deep space and solve the mysteries of the Universe.

Steering yoke

Independent wheel drive and suspension

FUTURE MOON BUGGY

In the early 1970s the Apollo astronauts rode their *LRV, Lunar Roving Vehicle*. Future Moon buggies will have solar panels to recharge their batteries for much longer trips.

Pressurized supply vehicle

Any Moon base will need an enclosed dome or container filled with air. Climate control inside must cope with an outside temperature range from minus 330°F (166°C) to plus 240°F (116°C).

The massive metal-and-glass domes of the Eden Project in Cornwall, England, house one of the world's largest "captive rain forests." Experience from these structures could help to plan Moon and Mars bases.

"Seemed like a good idea..."

The former USSR's N1 rockets tried to compete with the USA's Apollo Moon program. But they were too complicated and poorly tested. Four unmanned launches in 1969 to 1972 failed, and the USSR decided to focus on space stations.

LIFE ON MARS

More spacecraft have been sent to our nearest planet than any other. No signs of life are known. But there could be life on Mars in fifty years, when humans colonize the "Red Planet."

With plasma engines flaring, a nuclear-powered manned spacecraft might approach Mars orbit in 2035.

In 2008 the U.S. Phoenix lander proved there was water on Mars, frozen into ice in the Martian polar region.

SEEING RED

Even when Mars comes closest to Earth, the trip with today's technology takes more than three months. New kinds of propulsion may include bigger ion drives, fusion motors, and plasma engines to speed us on our way. Even so, the round-trip is at least one year.

Mars spacesuits would be based on those worn by astronauts today near Earth, for example, when fixing together parts of the ISS. They need air since Mars's thin atmosphere is mostly deadly carbon dioxide gas.

TERRAFORMING

On Mars, humans could "terraform"—alter conditions in their base area to be like those on Earth. It's not possible to take all the air, water, food, and other supplies for such an immense mission. So Martian soil, rocks, and minerals would be processed into water, building materials, and food farms for the Earthlings.

"Seemed like a good idea..."

In 1877 astronomer Giovanni Schiaparelli saw in his telescope "channels" on Mars. The idea grew that Martians had built water canals for farm crops—but it was a trick of the light.

Burning minerals in Martian rocks could create greenhouse gases to trap the Sun's heat, making the planet warm enough for humans.

MARS OUTPOST

The first bases on Mars would be sent fully constructed and equipped, probably taking over a year in a giant cargo spaceliner built in Earth orbit. People would travel once the base was safely in place.

Satellite relay

NASA's plan for a pioneer Mars base has a living pod and a working pod, with radio dishes for communication.

Viewport

Habitation pod

esa

Laboratory

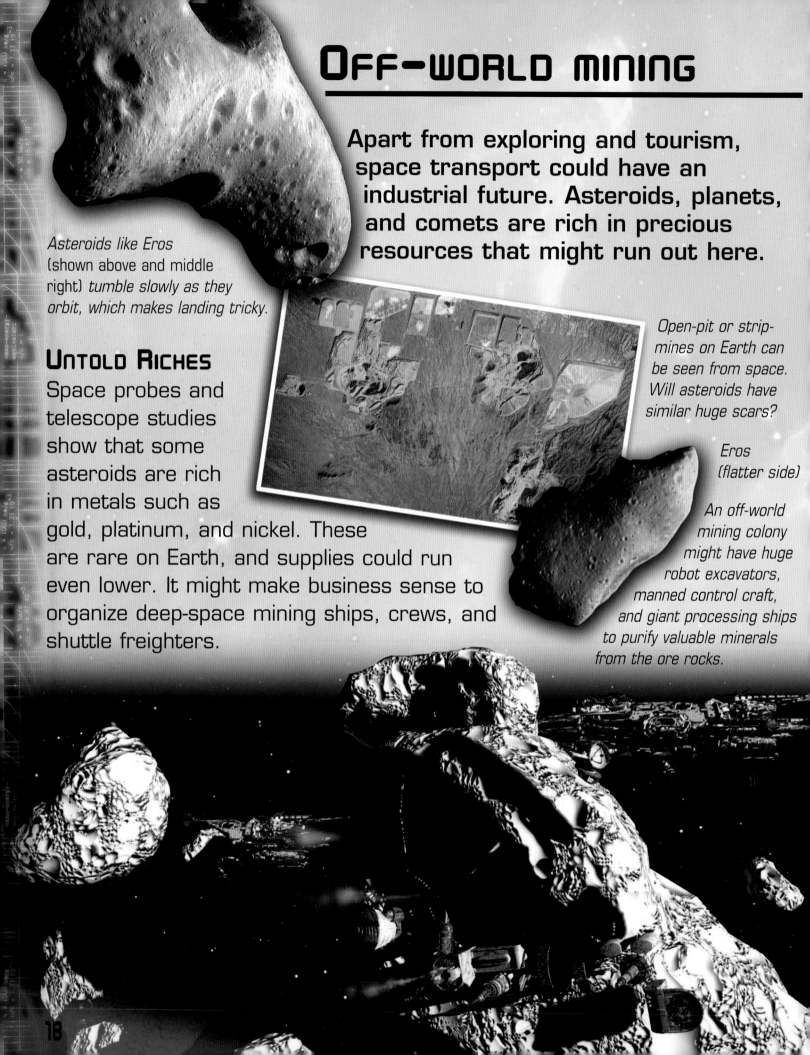

OFF-WORLD MINING

Apart from exploring and tourism, space transport could have an industrial future. Asteroids, planets, and comets are rich in precious resources that might run out here.

Asteroids like Eros (shown above and middle right) *tumble slowly as they orbit, which makes landing tricky.*

UNTOLD RICHES

Space probes and telescope studies show that some asteroids are rich in metals such as gold, platinum, and nickel. These are rare on Earth, and supplies could run even lower. It might make business sense to organize deep-space mining ships, crews, and shuttle freighters.

Open-pit or strip-mines on Earth can be seen from space. Will asteroids have similar huge scars?

Eros (flatter side)

An off-world mining colony might have huge robot excavators, manned control craft, and giant processing ships to purify valuable minerals from the ore rocks.

NEAs and MBAs

Some asteroids, known as NEAs (Near Earth Asteroids), orbit the Sun quite close to Earth. Getting there takes a few months. Thousands of Main Belt Asteroids, MBAs, orbit between Mars and Saturn, but trips there will take several years.

Helium-3 could be our main fuel for future energy, using nuclear fusion reactors being tested now. He3 is very rare on Earth but it might be mined on the Moon by 2050.

Japan's *H-2 TV* robot craft, which supplies the ISS, could be the basis for future designs 500 times bigger.

Unpressurized cargo module

"*Seemed like a good idea...*"

Asteroids in the Main Belt are often shown close together, jostling as they circle the Sun. They would be a great hazard for passing spacecraft, but ideal for mass mining. In fact most are hundreds of thousands of miles apart.

Guidance thrusters

Propulsion unit

Solar panels

ROBOT SPACE FREIGHTERS

Robot carriers could bring hundreds of tons of precious materials back to Earth. They would not need a pressurized area with crew life support and supplies. Manned pilot craft would check their approach and unloading.

SPACE PROBES

Every week, robots get smarter. Space probes are unmanned robot craft that are partly remote controlled from Earth, but also able to make decisions using their own computer "brain."

MERCURY PROBE

Mercury, closest planet to the Sun, is very hot! The *BepiColombo* probe is being designed now for launch around 2015 and arrival in 2020. By then, its computers and equipment will be ten years out of date.

Mercury magnetic field orbiter

The James Webb Space Telescope, *due in 2015, and successor to the* Hubble *telescope, will gather information for future probes.*

BepiColombo will aim for scorching Mercury.

Mercury planet orbiter

Transfer module

Ion engines

NEW HORIZONS

The space probe *New Horizons* is already in the future. It is due to reach dwarf planet Pluto, at the edge of our Solar System, in 2015. This is so far from Earth that, due to the time taken by radio signals, we will only know what the probe is doing more than five hours after it happens.

New Horizons should fly only 6,000 miles (9,700 km) from Pluto.

New Horizons' interplanetary cruise to Pluto takes nine years.

Deep Space Drives

Once in space, there is almost no force to slow down a spacecraft. So even a small engine or motor can give enough thrust. Ion drives push out atomlike particles called ions and need only a tiny power supply, which helps save fuel and weight, too.

Sun Probe

Solar Probe Plus should be within 3.7 million miles (6 million km) of the Sun in 2017. Even with shielding and protection, the heat would fry humans. The solar shield at the front gives some shade.

Carbon-composite solar shield

Several types of ion drives are being tested to find the most efficient and reliable design.

"Seemed like a good idea..."

In 2004 the Genesis *probe* flew past Earth to drop off a capsule of solar wind particles from deep space. A fault caused the capsule to crash-land at 200 mph (322 km/h).

Equipment stays in shield's shadow

The solar wind is a stream of fast particles heading away from the Sun. A probe with a vast fold-out solar sail could be blown along by it, like sailing ships blown by the wind.

LANDERS AND ROVERS

Flybys and orbiters to other worlds are OK, but close-up and personal is better. Landers touch down on the surface. Rovers travel on wheels or legs. What future secrets will they uncover?

The Mars twin rovers Spirit and Opportunity landed in 2004.

TOUCHDOWN!

Soft-touchdown methods are being improved for next-generation landers. With an atmosphere, a series of parachutes could work well. Without one, cushion-like airbags would allow the craft to come in at a shallow angle and bounce along. Or retro-rockets and thrusters can fire to slow the descent.

The six-legged Athlete rover is being developed for Moon-walking. It will step over boulders and carry up to half a ton.

MSL, MARS SCIENCE LABORATORY

At almost 1 ton, the *MSL* is the largest ever rover planned for the Red Planet. It aims to give a final answer to the age-old question: Is there, or was there ever, life on Mars?

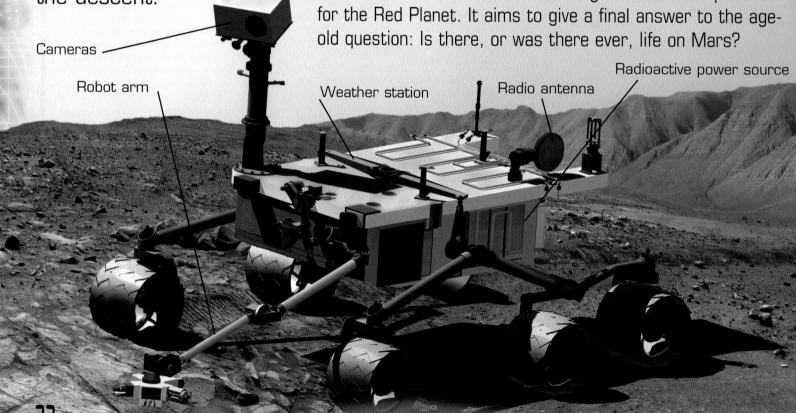

Cameras

Robot arm

Weather station

Radio antenna

Radioactive power source

The Rosetta probe should meet Comet Churyumov-Gerasimenko in 2014. It will release its trash can–sized Philae lander to land gently in the comet's tiny gravity.

"Seemed like a good idea..."

Beagle 2 was a lander on the 2003 probe Mars Express. Its three-part landing system of heat shield, parachutes, and airbags worked well in tests. But as it approached Mars, contact was lost.

POWER SOURCES

Some landers and rovers have solar panels, with rechargeable batteries for when it's dark. But they cannot work far from the Sun. An RTG, radioisotope thermoelectric generator, makes electricity from radioactive fuel even in the dark, but the fuel fades. Future power packs may use nuclear fusion.

The Scarab Moon lander is being tested on Earth. It drills holes 3 feet (90 cm) deep and crushes the rock samples to test them for minerals.

Saturn's moon Europa could have liquid oceans under its frozen surface. Robot submarines may search for life there.

Ares is a planned Mars robot aircraft. After unfolding from its mother ship, it would fly in the thin atmosphere and take survey photographs.

SPACE TOURISM

Time for a future vacation. Pack the clothes, camera, sunscreen, anti-cosmic ray hat, pressure suit, deep space survival kit... Space tourism may be the fashion fifty years from now, but probably you will have to be very rich.

Excalibur Almaz capsules are based on Russian TKS and Salyut designs. Launched by rocket, they will return to Earth with parachutes and retro-rockets.

The White Knight Two *mothercraft aims to launch* SpaceShipTwo *(center section) for suborbital Virgin Galactic flights with six travelers each time.*

THRILL SEEKERS

Back in 2001, U.S. engineer Denis Tito became the first paying space tourist. His 128 Earth orbits lasted over seven days and cost $20 million. What will attract the next generation of space visitors to pay huge costs? It would beat the neighbors' Pacific cruise, and the views are second to none!

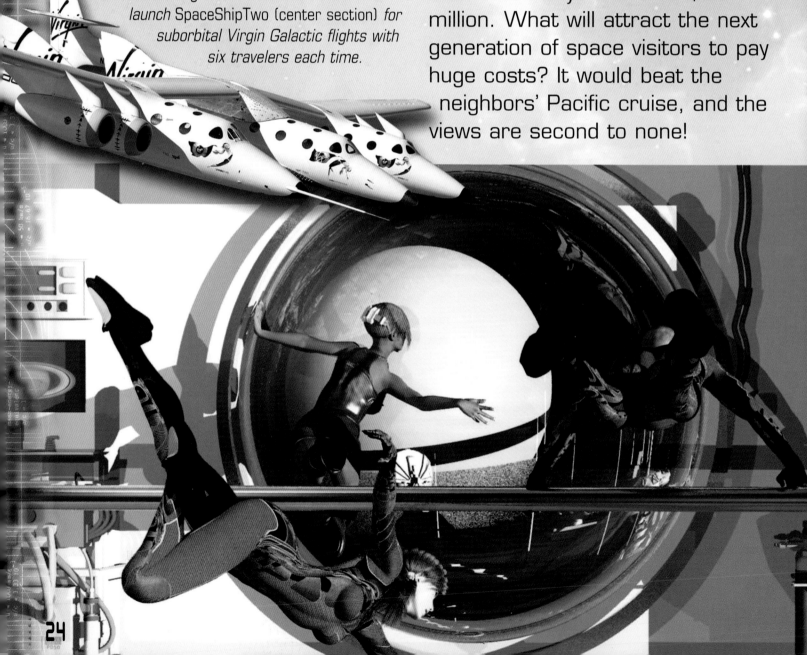

FFSC, Frequent Fliers Space Club

In space, medical care is a long way. Travelers will need detailed medical checks beforehand. The first trips, due soon, are simple up-and-down hops from Earth. Moon visits are a long way off, perhaps sometime later this century?

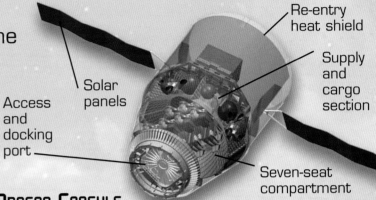

Re-entry heat shield

Solar panels

Access and docking port

Supply and cargo section

Seven-seat compartment

Armadillo Aerospace is testing vehicles that could carry six people (above), with vertical take-off and landing to save costs.

XCOR's two-seat Lynx rocket plane (below) could launch a satellite and take one passenger on the trip.

SpaceX Dragon Capsule

The *Dragon* capsule may mix sightseeing trips into orbit with docking at the *ISS* for crew and supplies. The interior design allows up to seven people, or 6 tons (5.4 t) of cargo, or a combination of these.

Maybe in the twenty-second century a Grand Planet Tour will take in the red glow of Mars, the giant swirling storms of Jupiter, Saturn's spectacular rings, and then a return trip in the deep sleep called suspended animation.

ALIENS AHOY!

Not only humans travel in space. Somewhere in our Galaxy, almost certainly there are other forms of life. A few may be far more advanced than us. They could be on their way here, right now!

THE FIRST MARTIANS?

A meteorite (space rock) found in Antarctica in 1984 came originally from Mars, probably knocked away by a bigger meteorite impact. Tiny shapes in it could be fossils of simple Martian life-forms.

Meteorite ALH84001

Possible fossil of Mars microbes

"Seemed like a good idea..."

In *The War of the Worlds (1898), science fiction author H.G. Wells describes advanced Martians in their walking war machines taking over Earth. But the invaders are killed by disease-causing Earth germs.*

KEEP IT CLEAN

No one knows what aliens may look like. But when spacecraft bring samples back to Earth, these must go through careful checks in "clean rooms" in case they carry unknown forms of life. Our craft are made perfectly clean for launch, too, in case they infect other worlds with Earthly micro-invaders.

The common Earth bug E. coli (right) *could wreak havoc on a world where life is just beginning.*

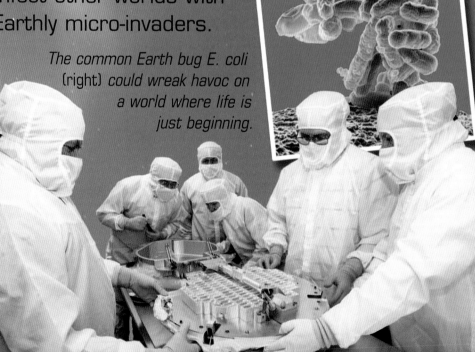

In 2006 the Stardust *space probe's return capsule, containing dust from Comet Wild 2, was opened under strict conditions.*

26

If aliens were
powerful enough to
reach Earth in giant
starships, our defenses
would be of little use.
However, they could be friendly.
They might simply be exploring our
Galaxy for simple beings with an early
stage of civilization—that is, ourselves.

INTERSTELLAR TRAVEL

The near future may bring trips to closer planets and their moons. But a century from now, technology we can hardly dream about could allow us to visit the stars.

ANTIMATTER DRIVE

Every tiny particle, such as the proton in an atom, has its anti-particle version. If two come together they destroy each other in a flash and produce energy. The antimatter drive will control this reaction to propel a craft at near light speed.

The Boussard *ramjet collects space dust, mainly hydrogen, using a vast magnetic scoop, and pushes it out of the rear fast to produce thrust.*

Crew chamber

Antiproton storage rings

Radiators

Reflecting shroud

Energy beam thruster (inside)

"Seemed like a good idea..."

Project Orion *was a 1960s design idea for a rocket with nuclear pulse propulsion. This was, in effect, many tiny nuclear explosions, like micro-atomic bombs, set off every second about 200 feet (60 m) behind the craft. These pushed against its rear shield.*

STAR DRIVES

After the Sun, our nearest star is Proxima Centauri. The fastest possible journey we can predict with tomorrow's science is about 100 years. Even at the speed of light, 186,000 miles (300,000 km) per second, it would take over four years. To make star travel possible, scientists will need some breathtaking new technologies.

No one knows what it might be like inside a wormhole or black hole. Future spacecraft would approach with care, but the pull of gravity could be too great.

Wormholes

In deep space there are astonishing objects and events that we struggle to understand, like black holes, quasars, neutron stars, and wormholes. The wormhole is a place where immense energy and gravity "fold" space itself into a double-ended funnel. A starship might enter at one end and pop out of the other in a split second—far across the galaxy.

29

LOOK FURTHER!

Compare our supersonic jets to the first slow, noisy aircraft. Likewise, space travel and transport have only just begun. The far future could see people flying across the galaxy and back before bedtime.

The new Orion craft being developed in the U.S.A. is based largely on the 1970s Apollo Mooncraft capsule. It is tried and trusted technology, rather than a great leap ahead.

The twenty-third century may see massive space cities orbiting Earth, with shuttle cruisers coming and going, and the Moon with bases in the background. Seeing how other technologies progress in just a few years, like computing and electronics, is this so far-fetched?

Glossary

Composites
Materials made from several substances like plastics, carbon or glass fibers, resins, and ceramics.

Gravity
The attraction or pulling force between all objects and all forms of matter, from an atom to a star.

Hybrid
A vehicle or craft with two forms of propulsion, such as a jet engine and a rocket motor.

Launch Vehicle
A craft or vehicle that lifts its load, such as a satellite or probe, into space. At present only rockets are powerful enough to do this.

Laser
A very pure, powerful, high-energy type of light energy. Laser = Light Emission by Stimulated Amplification of Radiation.

Maglev
Magnetic levitation, using magnetic forces of attraction (pulling together) or repulsion (pushing apart) to make an object or vehicle "float" or levitate.

Orbit
A curved path around and around an object, where straight-line forward speed is balanced and bent by the downward pull of gravity.

Solar Cells and Panels
Button-sized electronic devices that turn light into electrical energy. Many solar cells together in one large sheet are a solar panel (solar array).

Space
Where the air of Earth's atmosphere thins to become almost non-existent, leaving a vacuum (nothingness). By international agreement, space starts 62 miles (100 kilometers) above Earth's sea level.

Terraform
Alter conditions in an alien place to be more "friendly" like those on Earth, with oxygen and other gases in the atmosphere, rocks, and life—microbes, plants, and animals.

Turbine
A rotating shaft with angled fan-shaped blades or rotors, which spin around when gas or liquid flows past them, or turn to move gas or liquid.

Index